The Lion Kicks

The Lion Kicks

Poems

MATTHEW NINO AZCUY

RESOURCE *Publications* • Eugene, Oregon

THE LION KICKS
Poems

Copyright © 2018 Matthew Nino Azcuy. All rights reserved. Except for brief quotations in critical publications or reviews, no part of this book may be reproduced in any manner without prior written permission from the publisher. Write: Permissions, Wipf and Stock Publishers, 199 W. 8th Ave., Suite 3, Eugene, OR 97401.

Resource Publications
An Imprint of Wipf and Stock Publishers
199 W. 8th Ave., Suite 3
Eugene, OR 97401

www.wipfandstock.com

PAPERBACK ISBN: 978-1-5326-6201-0
HARDCOVER ISBN: 978-1-5326-6202-7
EBOOK ISBN: 978-1-5326-6203-4

Manufactured in the U.S.A.   10/26/18

For Christ himself
Lived, died, and was in hell
He could have destroyed mankind
But chose to heal
& to help
He chose to love
More than himself
He chose to be
He has risen, in me
These words;
Are belief
These verses
Are for the modern day
These verses are for you,
& for me
The lion kicks
The lion breathes
The Holy Spirit
In each piece

Contents

Chapter One
I am the way | 1

Chapter Two
I am the truth | 57

Chapter Three
& the life | 137

Chapter One
I am the way

The Lion Kicks

In the name of them
In the land of thee
From the shifting sand,
& in the hands of he

In the name of The Lord
The voice came to me
The Lion Kicks
While the baby;
breathes

I am the way

The comeback tale
The conquering of kings…
The pirates set sail
They found beauty
& they sing.

For in Christ himself
They are saved;
And in sync.

He changed their lives
Before the men;
Could even blink….

The Lion Kicks

I am a man
You are the truth
I am skin, muscles, and blood
But there is far more to you

A mysterious figure
The perfection, this vision
I suppose I cannot understand you

Just a poet,
who listened.

I AM THE WAY

To save all of man
From an oppressive state
The largest

The Lion of The Judah
The calm;
& the strongest

The Lion Kicks

The world in fear
The people trapped in darkness
The dirty child scared

Believing,
at its' hardest
The mark of the beasts
Hope was away
At its' farthest

But see over the hill with John
The archer angel.
Hits his target

I am the way

The sinners are saints
You awakened their peace
We are a puzzle of Christ
We all walk;
With one piece

The Lion Kicks

You can burn all the words
But not the spirit in me
Chills charge down my spine

An endless strength,
In defeat

I am the way

A roaring of Daniel
Goliath's allies retreat
You let swift victory come
To a feeble people
In need

The Lion Kicks

Born to a virgin
Not a birthing;
so neat

Your words and his verses
Almighty king,
I am free

I am the way

The Angels come
The drum line beats
I could never repay you.
But I surely can be…

A vessel of words
A message to be
The voice of millennium
A soldier
A seed

The Lion Kicks

The boy in his robes
Not a dollar he needs

There comes magic from his fingers
& there is an ocean,
beneath

I am the way

You are all that I love
A reflection of me
Seven pieces of gold
Spread all over;
The seas

The Lion Kicks

I am a vessel of truth
My mission still incomplete
I will speak of your love
Seven hundred heavenly

I will speak of your kingship
Of your excellency
I will exude of your beauty
Of your perfection;
 In me

I am the way

You accepted the peasant
You were welcoming me
You stood in the field
My shepherd waiting for me

You took a demon, and my hatred
& your hands;
set me free

The Lion Kicks

I cannot look at the light
I am unworthy to be
As I lay before your crown
I'll let your words,
flow in me.

I am the way

We will not surrender
The forever regime

We are the fighting survivors
Christ higher…
Achieved

The Lion Kicks

Ascension to the stars
A lift, to the cosmos

His servants took him home
The Messiah,
love hollowed

I am the way

I see three beings of faceless
A floating king
A glowing castle,
While the sunlight sings

I see green leaves against blue skies
As I lay under this tree

I consider my body
I am in awe at the beach
I love your golden sword
I am rejoicing,
for I see.

The Lion Kicks

He wrestled with Jacob
He parted,
The Red Sea

He came down from his angels
In order that hope;
May burn free

I am the way

The beast spit me out
Cracked my spine,
& defeated me

But my return to Jesus
Made me want to try again
For I believe.

The Lion Kicks

The apostles were taken
The men's hearts were forever altered and shaken
Their spirits alive
They were the chosen…
The awakened

I am the way

Far from divine
The evil of nations

A sorcerer from Babylon
The one who left;
The one taken

The one who was evil
Now humbled;
& now patient

The Lion Kicks

Paul of Tarsus
Divinely selected;
By truth

A vessel for the light
& a strong ally
For you

I am the way

I am not chosen
Not of Reuben, Nor Judah

But I know of your son
I know him
Let me through then

The Lion Kicks

I am not divine
I am a sinner
& that is proven

I caused pain, seven times seven
To many men;
Undeserving

I spoke a testament of lies
Now your lines
& your servant

I am the way

I have suffered long years,
Of a frightening dream
A dark monster with tentacles,
Sprouts his head from the sea

I panic at the destruction,
& the annihilation of me
It opens its mouth up,
& towers over me

I prepare to be eaten
I prepare for hellfire,
& heat.
But an angel steps in front
And the monster,
Just leaves…

The Lion Kicks

I am unworthy of him
To even pray on my knees
I am the most unholy one
I deserve the wrath,
& the beast

I am not even a hair
Or a blade of grass;
 To be seen…

But maybe in fact,
I can
Help even one man,
while he reads

I am the way

You are precious to him
& you never left me
In you I found comfort
The smiling carpenter,
At me

The Lion Kicks

You were perfect for him
There you stood;
One the sea

You gave fish to the people
You loved everything;
That you would see.

The being of hope
The light,
of Galilee

I am the way

A foreshadowing test
A hardship from you
A demonstration of holy
The miracles
The proof

You walked into my life
When I hated you

I was swimming in pain
But I saw a glimpse;
of the moon
For I was living in hate
But I was dreaming,
of you

The Lion Kicks

Lusting with demons
Crying out for you
You heard my soul screaming
You came looking and threw…

The baby boy on your back
I can breathe and I'm glad
I rejoice and I'm glad
I'm so glad,
That it's you

I AM THE WAY

The most imperfect
They may never believe
I'm only a poet who noticed
The change over me

It may never be golden
Never published
Nor seen

But my tongue is your weapon
& may the spirits,
Go free.

The Lion Kicks

God is here
God does not give up
Love is an even avenue,
& his love is enough

We wander aimlessly
Curious why aren't happy and rough
When you want something bad
You must give The Lord…
What he wants.

I am the way

"You're the worst at everything"
What my cousins would say to me
But victory is had here already
For I am a man;
who believes very heavy

Seventy-seven times
Victory will wash over me
For my messiah will return
Almighty king of the heavens,
& the sea

The Lion Kicks

I am 1994
I am reborn a new breed
There was an ink cylinder between my skins…
Placed into my hands;
For these

In the mirror I see
One former drug addict and pervert
Hooked on narcotics and weed….

As my vitals collapsed
A vision I'd see
A clear picture of Christ

Throughout my suffering rage
I saw his physicality
& I was never
the same

He created man
In all the vast pigments
He made an array of human emotion
& showed mortal men visions

He took his own thoughts
& painted with an according precision

He breathed life into us all
& molds infants
In the women

I am the way

The sun in April
The miracles in May
The love in July
The canyons,
& the lakes

The valleys and structure
The hours of day
The leaves of autumn
The blood red
In his name

The Lion Kicks

I cried tears
It is pain to believe
My lids drift aback
I see your face in the heat

I got on my shins
I begged for some relief
& knowing that one day I would

You one day walked
next to me

I guess we're stuck with one another
I guess I'm a part of the team
The believers of the century
The Christians
& me

I AM THE WAY

Israel has changed
In the castles they sleep
Bathsheba bathing on her roof
For King David to see
Her wet and beautiful black hair
Her dark skin hard to breathe
You proved there is nothing you couldn't do
& that all men,
can be redeemed.

The Lion Kicks

A lineage of champions
That David was given
The God of Israel is coming
The children;
& the children are christened

A love everlasting
For with The Lord ignorance is forgiven
Son of God, King of Man
His father's kingdom
he was given.

I am the way

David and Solomon
Moses & Israel
Abraham and Isaac
Hagar & Ishmael

The living examples…
The breathed into proof
A stunning new sample
A higher consciousness
A truth.

A peace like no other
May you shower us with love
May you watch over;
& hover.

The Lion Kicks

He could have picked the royals
The famous and the rich…
He went to the rejects
The bastards
The outcasts
The losers, and the witch

He called sinners to repentance
The damnation kissed

He loved those whom had none
He loved the beautiful
The kids.

I am the way

Who was this man?
A glitch in our history
The scholars agree
The earths greatest mystery

Christ,
The messiah
The Son of God
The Lion

He cannot be fathomed
Nor comprehended or understood…

He is the best of all planners
A miracle,
the good

The Lion Kicks

Darkness and bloodshed
Jesus and the rams-head
Prince of light versus darkness

Determination;
For the broken

I am the way

I may suffer more
Bring on the rain
The Son of God is with me
To wipe the blood,
& my pain.

The Lion Kicks

The beach of Galilee
Twelve witnesses chosen
Do you think them to be crazy?

They saw him rise
They watched him crowned
The awoken.

I am the way

You say the world cannot change
I attempt it with each poem spoken

Just because you gave up on the earth
Doesn't mean I will
You're broken….

The Lion Kicks

Stay determined
Have purpose
God is wisdom
God is learning.

Give alms
Give praises
God the Father

The exalted…
& the famous.

I am the way

Open the gates
Joshua is lead
Tribe of Abraham
We come of the same seed

We fight & we kill
We all fail to see
The Glory of God
May he give us all peace.

May he give sobriety to families
May he reattach,
Each piece…

The Lion Kicks

She smokes on the corner
She drinks
To find peace

She gets high,
To numb her heart
God's daughter…
His art

She worries he doesn't love her
But he feels her
He's not far…

I am the way

The Baptist in prison
Friends of Judas
The ridicule of God's people
There is still strength to be seen

We scream through the torment
We sing
For our King

The Lion Kicks

I see a cathedral
I see the flames ignite
I see soldiers surrounded
But soldiers who fight…

I see protestants disputing
& the Catholics' fighting
I pray these words defuse them…
The conflicts rising.

Brothers in arms
An armada colliding
Comradery falling
A family
One dying

I am the way

You can cut my arms off
Perhaps chainsaw my tongue
The devil has lost
& God has won…

This is not a challenge
For I am too weak

I follow The Lord
For the beast,
they have beat

The Lion Kicks

They wore symbols of Christ
They laughed at the locusts
They are the twelve determined
The awakened;
The focused.

I am the way

Cigarettes
Wine & weed

I almost died once
But I was given one chance,
& I was set free.
December twenty third,
Twenty sixteen

Seven blinding lights
Heaven sent
Unto me…

The Lion Kicks

It was a roman bell
An angel's chorus
Light healed my body
The Lord has a job for us

He has a great purpose
For all of creation
I am Nino Azcuy
A former ally,
of Satan

Chapter Two
I am the truth

The Lion Kicks

I spent minutes
Delivering the message

I spent my own money
I want us all to have blessings

I read of Moses and Paul
I was never the same
I laid at Stone Hedge in awe…

I was a junkie
A sex addict…
Until I met Christ

A love so splitting
It cut into my veins
Like a sharp blade
The white knife.

For the love of Jehovah
To have sun
To dance

To laugh with our family
To have joy
A new chance…

To feast on inner peace
The Holy Spirit,
In his hands.

I am the truth

I don't mean to be extreme
Or offensive to you
I only tell of what I have seen
I heard a message
For you…

I see a reptile
A black energy
& sad painful youth

But I feel a Holy Ghost
Let him in-
side of you

The Lion Kicks

God has rules
Of what is good for you

The only way you fail
Is to give away truth
To value money over prayer
To exchange God's advice
To hurt and to do,
evil on the planet.
Doors not meant for you…

Live a clean and sober life
God only aims;
To help you.
Live a life filled with Christ
He was sent here,
As proof…

I saw men die of heroin
Their shameful abuse
Families covered in pain…
I see pornography consume

I hear the people exclaim
The Gospel wasn't truth
That the words of Christ are of myth…
I suppose ignorance is peace
I suppose blindness
Is bliss…

I am the truth

I remember an eve
When God's light went away
Sunlight was snuffed,
& the tide stayed the same…

Clouds covered men
Blue water turned to gray
Dead animals on the grounds
The heart of man,
had lost faith

The Lion Kicks

The pen is mightier than the sword
I don't hear your skepticism
The sellouts,
The whores…

I serve a being
So much higher and more

If God has forbidden something
Then it is final…
From the Lord

I am the truth

Orgies and gambling
Moral lines scraped to gray
I saw black and white gone
I saw that eve,
On today….

The Lion Kicks

They say he has no eyes
Though his vision is plain
He reads spirits and hearts
He judges fairly
The exalted and praised

For the land of the free
For the home of the brave
Come home to America

Come to us
Come to save.

I am the truth

Cyrus The King
The Persian Empire's great

The destroy Satan's Babylon
Rescue Israel
Through the gates

God controls all
He seals all our fates
God makes thunder in the clouds
& lightning,
hit the lakes.

The Lion Kicks

Joseph Smith
Jim Jones
& all the false prophets

This is the lion's cry of war
False messiah's
& our targets'

I am the truth

We will not worship your God
We cannot be taken
We cannot be bought
Sold off, nor shaken

Faith in The Lord
We are the beautifully awakened

We are the soldiers of white lightning
We are the forever
The mistaken

The Lion Kicks

Throw us into the flames
Go on then Nebuchadnezzar

You will worship the God of Abraham
God of Israel
In one second.

I am the truth

I don't claim to be
A walking apostle
But make no mistake
This work is far from imposter

I am connected
Both beating and selected

I am the change
I am in Christ
In perfection

The Lion Kicks

Lost in the sand
They spoke
"I am with him"

An agnostic transformed
Give me water
Give me wisdom…

I am the truth

Fear is gone
I will ember these words
In the age of atheism
May these symbols be heard
Heaven's new patriot

I care for Christ
Thy kingship come…

I was nervous of their opinions
Now I fear no man
Not one

The Lion Kicks

Seven hundred poems
For the Lion of Judah
For King David and Pilate
For the ones that knew him

Oh Abraham & Isaac
May the light flow through them
Give the boy who denied and lied

The Pen
& the truth
The way,
and the you.

I am the truth

The redemption of Saul
The black seed of Tarsus
The lord challenged him greatly
He was the devoted
The hardest

The grown man taken and consumed
The journey
The harvest

The Lion Kicks

Spill ink onto canvas
If you say you are true
I don't know what God's plan is
But I know he loves you

He adores the birds
He watches his winds
He loves every strand of hair
and each
Of our kids…

I am the truth

You must kill me to stop
The words and the truth
As you see I'm not scared…

I met Jesus,
Who are you?

The Lion Kicks

I am a sniper of Christ
A disciple of truth
A new wave of triumph
A Sinner
Like you.

I am the truth

Jeremiah's to blame
A prophet delivered the message
I was given these lines
To remind them
Of blessings.

The Lion Kicks

I expect detractors
I expect critics of my religion

Behold the Holy Trinity
& in my tongue,
there is vision.

I am the truth

This will only work
For those of them who listen

Snow from the angels
& the love
During Christmas.

The Lion Kicks

Not a cloud on the horizon
I must be pleasing him
I stretch my flesh to the sky
I am weak
 I am needing him.

I am the truth

Trapped in hatred
Your family suffers
If you've had enough
Saul's eyes were too covered

There is an answer
Low and behold
Change your ways today,
and come boldly to his throne

Guilt is an emotion
Not yet understood
We are wired for God
We are meant,
for what's good.

The Lion Kicks

Pharaoh
A hardened heart

A glowing metropolis
In the dark

I am the truth

Sorry for delay
My Lord I am late
I worshipped other gods
I would sin and seal fates

Then came one day
You made me a promise
To put lights on my name

When I gave,
all you wanted.

The Lion Kicks

Now comes my time
I pray that I pass the test

I pray I can keep my promise
because God always
keep his…

I am the truth

All I can write
I think I can manage it
Like the dust in my mind
Like the breath that I manifest

My clay hands
Molding a bird
It pales in comparison
My works are obscure…

Lifted through faith
Like a studded golden chariot
He deserves all the praise
Too much…
I can't handle it.

The Lion Kicks

A mission to save
A journey to please us
I suppose I may die
When I reach,
King Jesus.

I am the truth

"More than a prophet"
He musters the light in the dark

Raised from Gods locket
& made,
from his heart.

The Lion Kicks

He loved us so much
He made the angels sing
He gave bread to the sinners
He gives us love in the spring…

He makes freedom for man
In the Land of Milk & Honey
He is the everlasting thing…
Above fame
Above money

I am the truth

The Son of God
A beautiful cancer
His words spread like venom
Christ is the cure
& the answer.

The Lion Kicks

I call out for my brothers
The ones in Jesus
I am alone and outnumbered
No one to discuss all my feelings

Something has suffered
Someone is healing
My life and my mother
The glue then
Between us.

I am the truth

The Lord worked
He went about his business
For man to see God
The royal religion

The magic in hand
The mountainous vision
The blind man is healed
& given vision.

The Lion Kicks

I used to have a name
A code on government pages
Then the trinity came
I am a soldier
A faceless....

I AM THE TRUTH

I don't need praise anymore
No earthly veneration

I write to inspire
To awaken;
The generations.

The Lion Kicks

After a moment with The Lord
I don't see any else

I want to write
& inspire

To guard them
against hell…

I am the truth

The Lord does provide
The sustenance for me
The Lord will then give me
All that I need

The Lord will be sure
I have enough to be
I can give them the words
I can pray
On these knees.

The Lion Kicks

The Lord came down
Many saw him not
Let his light into your bones
Before the calcium rots…

I am the truth

Matthew
Mark
Luke
& John

Mary and Joseph
The one who carried them all
The chosen few
The proud to serve you
Before the castles and money

The ones in cloaks
Close to you…

The Lion Kicks

I have returned
Upon sheer principle
I am with Christ
The one stunning visual

I am a King
In another land

I am a general
With wisdom in hand…

I am the truth

Come and get me
I am invulnerable
I am a vessel,
A carrier

A train uncontrollable
The unkillable
The invincible
The light;
The invisible…

The Lion Kicks

Christ's ascension
We are an empire
We are the royalty
The white fire…

The cure to hate
A flaming chariot
A love that feeds
On the betrayal of Judah,
& Iscariot….

I am the truth

You didn't see it
The comeback
The vision

I was chosen for this
I am the decision
For my loyalty came
Divine sets of visions

I saw a sword in the rock
& I chose to lift it
I am the fighting chance
I am the sinner
I am the gifted…

The Lion Kicks

You came back
Seven scrolls
Seventy legions
With only one goal…
Kill the demon

Save the people
The young and the old
Rescue man kind
From the snake
The souls sold…

I am the truth

You call us crazy
I call us gifted
You call us stupid
But I call it lifted

We are the fighters
We are the Christian
Under Jesus
One fight
One religion…

The Lion Kicks

I grow weary of the same
The pain inside of the mundane of days
I crave love in my heart
I wish to laugh
& to pray

I want to dance
In the rain

I want to last
To sing his praise
I see the beach
He is the way
I wake up,
I love the day
I love you Lord
I hope always…

Music is dull
Food has lost taste
The sky became black
& the trees fly away…

Let Israel in
Let the trees become green
Let the sun smile down
Let the winds become serene
God can be a great friend
Or a nightmare, a bad dream

God can stretch his mighty hands

I am the truth

Or he can punish,
those who leave…

The Lion Kicks

Friendship yes indeed…
A two-way street
We support one another
Except he doesn't need me

I am a servant to them
One, two, and three
Seven hundred ways
God of Israel
God of me…

I am the truth

I could have turned back
I could have swallowed defeat
I could have blasphemed his name
I could suffer and be weak

Or I could configure a way
To make his gifts be seen
There never came one day
When he gave up,
on me…

The Lion Kicks

Christ is the light
In an ocean of darkness
He is a glimpse of the moon
When I am drowning in the waves,
of the darkest

I AM THE TRUTH

I would show the world
That Christ is the way
He is the answer
The redemption

He is peace
The perfection

The Lion Kicks

I will admire
With pure passion
on each page

The Holy Spirit will hear him
I will shout
Out his name....

I am the truth

I came down from Christ
To suffer & know pain
I had to understand
I had to feel,
to help save…

The Lion Kicks

Let it go
Let hatred tumble off my shoulders

I look at your moon
Your planets and typhoons

The Lords galaxy

The king
of solar systems and space
I won't attempt to fathom
I will accept my destiny,
& my fate…

I am the truth

The stairway to Heaven
Golden steps from The Lord….

He came to Jacob in the sand
He handed Israel…
Seven swords

The Lion Kicks

My body became frail
Diseased and weak
My body was destroyed
But a victory beneath

I put on seven tons of muscle
I am a miracle
A new leaf…

I AM THE TRUTH

A seventh shot at life
A renewal
of my dreams…

The Lion Kicks

God has spoken
Give them grapes and their bread…

Let the servants have my words
Put the letters,
In their heads…

I AM THE TRUTH

God is like water
Thin, all encompassing
Sublime inside the skin cells and blood

He drops tears full of hope
He fills our stomachs up with food
And breathes love into our nose…

The Lion Kicks

God loves the beaches in Cuba
The streets of Bangladesh
The pollution of Hong Kong
He is life,
& death...

The mountains of Russia
Man came of his breath

God is love & the clouds
It is good
God has said

I am the truth

I want to be King
I want the crown of David
I want the glory and castle
I want to be lifted
The famous…

The Lion Kicks

Chasing what is empty
I was ungrateful and heinous

I am a member of Christ Jesus
I am an ally
A faceless

The new Israel made
The conservative shoulder
I believe in the Angels
& The Lord,
is my boulder…

I am the truth

I am a tax collector
In twenty eighteen
I am a luster
A heathen
I am a demon
Who believes…

The Lion Kicks

God is like a new tree
Filled with life, colors, and art.
His seed is firm in the soul
It grows and sprouts outwards,
from our hearts…

I am the truth

Father, Son,
& Holy Spirit

At the very minimum
May I be redeemed,
with these lyrics…

The Lion Kicks

I lost the first round
I drowned
I lost many

But my forces have regrouped
Heavens Angels
I have plenty…

I am the truth

God is like the wind
Always eager to push

God is like the sun
Ready to expose
And show truth

God is in the sands
He works through many

Erupting from the bottom
We are scattered,
and grow weary…

The Lion Kicks

The staff of Moses
God carries in you
He sent down stone tablets
Cosmic symbols
& proof

I am the truth

The horn of Joshua
The unthinkable victory
A weak tribe exalted
Israel's enemies
In misery…

The Lion Kicks

Heartbreak
Madness…
Suffering & pain

I would work
To believe

I made a deal
To have strength

I am the truth

They want my words demolished
For the demons
Unfitting

But Gods servants will reign as princes
My words cut;
a white splitting

The Lion Kicks

Like the infiltrating of an atom
Like deep sea fishing
Seventy-seven needles puncture in
& inject what is missing…

The Lords guidance
His sons divine mission
His perfection made clear
The divine
The new visions…

I am the truth

God is like a star
A light binding and ever giving
Hope is in the sky
Hope and love,
are now winning…

The Lion Kicks

Praise be The Lord.
I see faith
& I preach

Creator of the mammoths
The lands
Our hands & the sea…

Bringer of rain
He cures the diseased

He gives us hope for each day
With the faith
We believe…

I am the truth

A man said to me
"you neglect your reason"
He may be right
But I delight
In believing…

The Lion Kicks

The Lord is my reason
I lay under the tree
I see their sun light and I'm breathing
I am safe
I am free

I AM THE TRUTH

I hunt so many
I have taken from plenty

God is persistence
Not afraid to start
From beginning.

The Lion Kicks

A crazy teen
There was a time for that
For naivety
& disbelief...

With the Lord
That time is done
I was rescued
I was saved
I lay
With the sun...

Chapter Three

& the life

The Lion Kicks

& though have I suffered,
May I always believe…
I may be happy in another land…
across seas.

& THE LIFE

They went through the motions
But they never believed
Loveless souls for parents
You shouldn't parent children indeed

The Lion Kicks

Perhaps a test
An earthly fulfillment
I can't understand twenty-three years of hardship
I can't understand…
Help me Jesus

& THE LIFE

Nothing works out
What am I missing?
Is Christ my executioner?
Is this defeat that I'm kissing?
What is the problem?
A death so poetic
& so fitting…

Hell is on earth
It's lonely
It's cold
It's rough and it's splitting

You put your everything into success
Nothing in return
No love,
& no giving.

I prepare for a quest
In the land of fruits and honey
I pray I passed my test
May something good happen to me

Christ I need a miracle
You don't seem to listen to me
Christ why do you always help bad people?
Is it grace?
So confusing…

The Lion Kicks

Lord what must I do
For you to hear my prayer
What can I do to prove?
& to peel back the layers

It must be in front
One last missing piece
Enough money for success
& enough bread
To have peace....

& THE LIFE

I lost my first love
When I close my eyes
I imagine a reset
As if we woke up in bed again
2012
Before the preaching

Am I on a divine mission?
Or am I losing my sanity?
I'm chasing the religion
But will this chase be calamity?
Is this pursuit worth it?
Does it ever stop hurting?
May the Lord heal my pain
I am bruised
I am burning.

The Lion Kicks

They said don't add to these pages
May the additive burn
May the package who carries blasphemy
Feel hellfire and burn…

But what if the man
Didn't realize his deeds were bad

What if I'm a man writing poems
What if I'm not….
That bad?

& THE LIFE

Can the Lord forgive a man?
Who wanted to show them?
Who wanted to speak of good things?
Who didn't try to control them?

Who embraced all his pain,
and wore the garments of his sin

Who never played games
Who just wanted to win

To destroy those who called him names
Is he selling life short?
Does the Lord work against him?
Is he of Babylon?
Is he a whore?

The Lion Kicks

I wasn't trying to upset you
I wasn't trying to fit in.
I was trying to fight
But I guess I didn't win

I guess these words aren't needed.
You don't need a new soldier
You're king of the solar…
You are King
I am no one.

& THE LIFE

The wine
The seas
The camels and bees
The honey and fruits
The metals and trees

The environment is ours
& on us you had mercy
The meek will inherit the earth
The human
The unworthy.

www.ingramcontent.com/pod-product-compliance
Lightning Source LLC
Chambersburg PA
CBHW050826160426
43192CB00010B/1911